THIS BOOK BELONGS TO

....

HODDER CHILDREN'S BOOKS
First published in Great Britain
in 2026 by Hodder & Stoughton Limited

Text and illustration copyright © Hodder and Stoughton Limited 2026

All rights reserved.

A CIP catalogue record for this book is available
from the British Library.

ISBN: 978-1-444-98376-0
E-book ISBN: 978-1-444-98377-7

1 3 5 7 9 10 8 6 4 2

Printed in China

Hodder Children's Books
An imprint of Hachette Children's Group
Part of Hodder & Stoughton Limited
Carmelite House
50 Victoria Embankment
London EC4Y 0DZ

An Hachette UK Company
www.hachette.co.uk
www.hachettechildrens.co.uk

The authorised representative in the EEA is Hachette Ireland,
8 Castlecourt Centre, Castleknock Road, Castleknock,
Dublin 15, D15 XTP3, Ireland
(email: info@hbgi.ie)

THE EASTER STORY

RETOLD BY
BROOKE DAVIS

ILLUSTRATIONS BY
AG JATKOWSKA

HODDER

Jesus, the Son of God, was beloved by everyone he met. Everywhere he went, he helped people, blessed them and performed miracles. More and more people learned of his teaching. Everyone wanted to meet him, to be with him and to feel the joy of God's love.

Everyone, that is, except for the most powerful people in the land. From kings and Roman rulers to priests and temple leaders, many people were jealous of Jesus and how popular he was with the people.

Jesus knew that he was in danger, but he rode courageously into Jerusalem on a donkey. The crowds cheered, waving palm leaves, and calling out, "Hosanna! Hosanna in the highest!" as they praised him.

The whole city was excited, but this made the leaders even angrier. Jesus bravely told the people that their leaders were as sneaky as snakes. He knew that they pretended to be good, even though they had evil in their hearts.

Jesus stopped at the house of his friends, Mary Magdalene, Martha and Lazarus. Jesus had raised Lazarus from the dead, and the family were very grateful to him for this miracle. To show her gratitude, Mary washed his feet and rubbed them with a precious, expensive ointment.

One of Jesus' twelve apostles was called Judas. Judas was angry that Mary had wasted something so expensive, but Jesus said, "Mary has done something kind for me, and she will always be remembered for her generosity."

Then Judas did a terrible thing: he went to the city leaders and promised to bring Jesus to them in exchange for thirty silver coins.

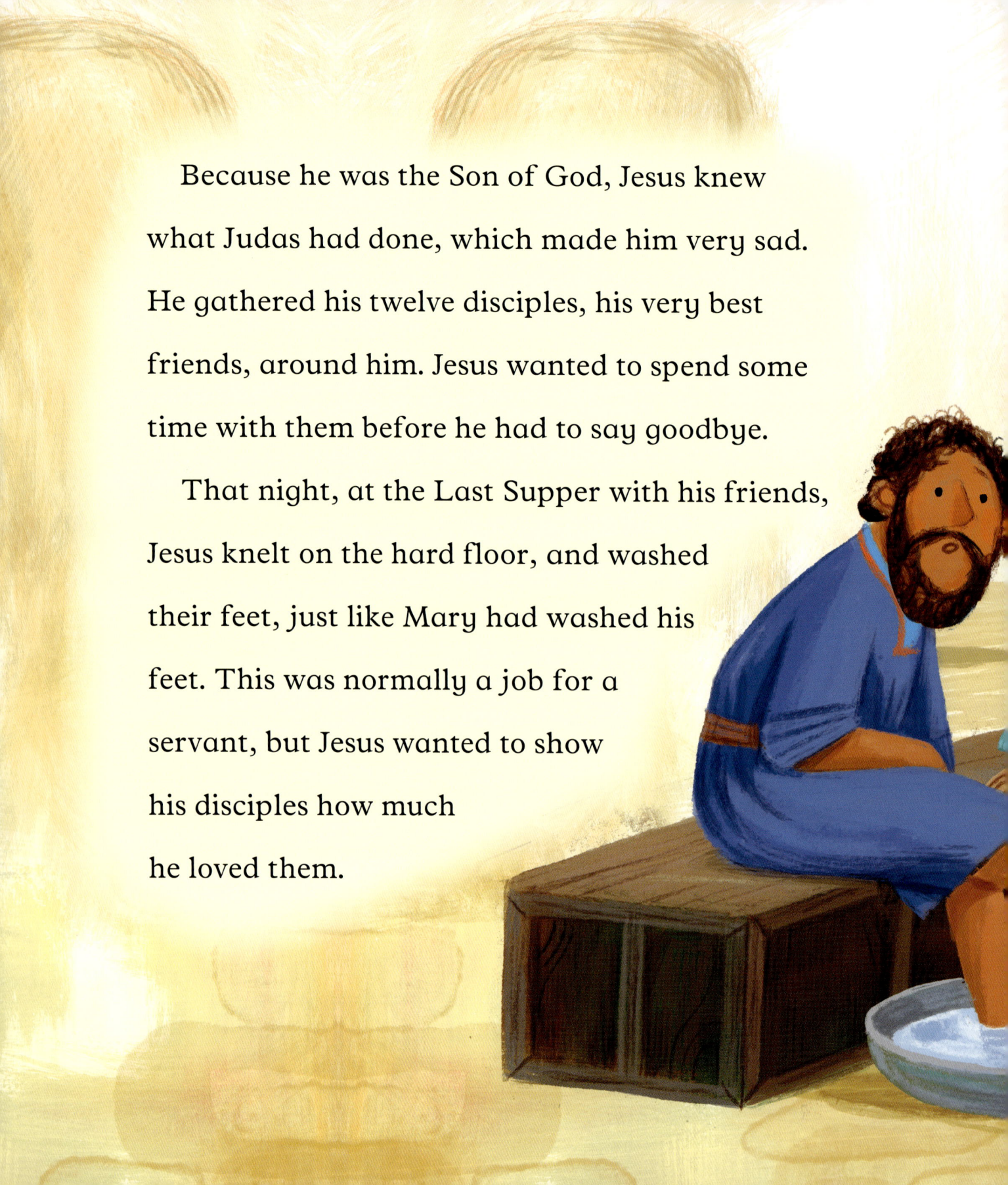

Because he was the Son of God, Jesus knew what Judas had done, which made him very sad. He gathered his twelve disciples, his very best friends, around him. Jesus wanted to spend some time with them before he had to say goodbye.

That night, at the Last Supper with his friends, Jesus knelt on the hard floor, and washed their feet, just like Mary had washed his feet. This was normally a job for a servant, but Jesus wanted to show his disciples how much he loved them.

Jesus asked them to remember him: "When you eat your bread, imagine it is my body; when you drink your wine, imagine it is my blood. With these symbols, you will remember me forever, even when I am gone."

Jesus said goodbye to them with a heavy heart, for he knew that his friends could not protect him. He felt sad, and very lonely.

Jesus went alone to the Garden of Gethsemane and prayed to God. He was frightened. "Dear Father," he said, "I know that you will care for me, even though I will be killed tomorrow. I know that you love me, even though I will suffer. I am your son, and I have lived my life to please you. I hope that you will bring me to your side, in heaven."

Later that night, Judas stepped forward and kissed Jesus' cheek, which was the sign he had agreed with the bad leaders . . . and Jesus was arrested at once. Jesus looked sadly at Judas, at the man who had once been his friend, but who had betrayed him for a few coins.

Because there were no laws then as there are now, which protect people from unfairness, the wicked leaders decided that this good, gentle man would be killed.

The next day Jesus was hung on a cross alongside two thieves. He called out to God, "Forgive them, for they do not know what they are doing." Even when he was dying, Jesus showed love and forgave his enemies.

That afternoon, the sky went dark with God's great sadness, and Jesus died.

Jesus' friends lovingly took his body down from the cross and brought him to a tomb. There they carefully washed his wounds, even though he could not feel their touch, and gently kissed him goodbye. Then they rolled a big boulder in front of the tomb, and slowly walked back home.

Three days later, Jesus' friends Peter, John and Mary went to visit the grave. But when they got to the tomb, the boulder had been rolled away and it was empty – Jesus was gone! Peter and John were puzzled and went back home, while Mary stayed by the tomb, weeping with sadness. When she looked up, there stood two angels, as well as another man.

The man said kindly to Mary, "Why are you weeping? It is I, Jesus." He had risen from the dead!

Mary cried out with joy and ran to tell Jesus' disciples the wonderful news. His friends could hardly believe their eyes when they saw him, but their hearts were full of joy at God's greatest miracle.

Jesus stayed with his friends for forty days. Then one day, Jesus knew that it was time to leave them once more. He asked his disciples to promise to spread the word of God, and of course they agreed.

Then Jesus rose up to Heaven, once more by God's side.

Two angels appeared and told Jesus' disciples that Jesus would come again one day. His friends were overjoyed that he would return, and gave thanks to God.

NOTE FOR PARENTS

Here is where you can find this story in the New Testament:

New Testament | Matthew | Chapters 26-28

New Testament | Mark | Chapter 14-16

New Testament | Luke | Chapters 22-24

New Testament | John | Chapter 17-20